D1649933

Smoothie Diet

The Smoothies Recipe Book for a Healthy
Smoothie Diet, Including Smoothies for
Weight Loss and Optimum Health

Jarrod Becker

Table of Contents

Smoothie Basics and You

What is a smoothie? What makes it so much different from any other type of drink on the market? The biggest difference of course is that the smoothie is a blended drink, containing a number of different ingredients. While some smoothies are designed for taste, others are designed for health. Then again, you always have the in-between ground wherein you can have both taste AND health benefits!

Before you get started with your smoothing making adventure, it would be within your best interest to make sure you have the right tools on hand. The most common items you are going to need, and find in common with all of the recipes in this book, is a blender. While most smoothies can be made with any blender, you will need to make sure you have a particularly high end one if you are going to be making vegetable smoothies. It can be a bit difficult to blend broccoli and carrots properly, and as you know, even a juicer might not get it right the first ten times.

A smoothie is comprised of a few different ingredients, and once you look over the recipes named in this book, you might even try experimenting with a few of your own. The most important thing to remember however, is that while smoothies taste great, they are intended to sustain your health and even get you to a better place in your life. That being said, make sure you are using healthy ingredients, and most importantly, make sure you are using the right smoothie for the right occasion. Some are suitable for breakfast, some are great for lunches, and others are perfect for that energy boost you need first thing in the morning. Then again, some smoothies are better for the all important liver purge.

Common Smoothie Ingredients:

Chocolate
Peanut Butter
Fruit
Frozen Fruit
Crushed Ice
Honey
Syrup
Milk
Yogurt
Soy Milk
Whey Powder
Green Tea

Though these are some of the most common ingredients, we don't recommend that you add them all at once. Instead, we are going to provide you a few great recipes in the following categories:

Fruit smoothies

Green Smoothies

Breakfast Smoothies

Energy Smoothies

Before we get into the different smoothie recipes, let's talk a bit about the detox diet along with the function of the liver. Before you attempt to perform a liver detox however, it would be within your best interest to get to know the liver and understand just why it needs detox from time to time.

Liver Detox and You

Every system, whether organic or mechanical will need some type of filter. In the human body, the liver serves as the primary filter, and it is virtually impossible to maintain good health without it. The problem however is that we tend to abuse our 'filter' over time, and it will lead to some type of illness. If you want to stop this illness from occurring, there are a few things you need to do. First of all you need to make sure you remove all the excess fat from the liver. In addition to that, bile needs to flow free, and toxic waste must be filtered out. If possible, gallstones should be dissolved and passed while regenerating damaged cells.

Many people consider the liver to be the most important organ in the body, but when it comes to healthcare it is ironically forgotten. With 200 separate identified functions, the liver is vital for regulating and breaking down different substances inside the body. These functions include, but are not limited to the following:

Fat Storage Regulation
Blood Cleansing
Discharge of Waste
Energy Production
Hormone Balance
Tissue Regeneration(Self)
Storage of Vitamins and Minerals
Metabolize Alcohol
Manufacture New Proteins
Produce Immune Factors
Remove Bacteria from Blood Stream
Manage Chemicals

While the average person might not give the liver a second thought, there are many in the medical profession who are of the opinion that a great number of diseases can actually be prevented completely if the liver is in working order. An unhealthy liver will be like a gateway to all sort of disease and should be corrected as quickly as possible.

Harm can come to the liver in a number of different ways. One such event might involve an excess of protein in the diet, while you might also find that simple carbohydrates do their share of harm. The more fat you have stored in the liver, the harder it is for the liver to actually function. This is something for you to think about the next time you choose to eat an entire plate of fried chicken.

Overeating is another issue and serious temptation that we all face. Not only is overeating hard on the figure, it also provides too much enzyme deficient food and stresses the liver. One thing that pharmaceutical companies likely won't tell you is that drug residue is typically left in the body after medications have been taken. This of course is second only to the inflammation caused by alcohol and other chemicals. The icing on the cake is a lack of exercise, which forces the liver to do elimination work typically performed by the skin and lungs.

Some of the most common problems in the liver can include digestive problems, constipation, low energy output, hay fever, diabetes, obesity, and even hypertension. As you can see, these are issues that you really want to avoid! But what do you do about it? The liver, fortunately, is an organ that is more than capable of repairing itself if you give it a chance. In spite of this, you need to do your best to keep healthy, and ensure that your liver is capable of functioning normally.

How do you know what sort of diet to use? As a rule, you should try to diet depending on the severity of the illness you are facing. In other words, the sicker you are, the more you need to clean up your diet. In any case, it is strongly recommended that you do a liver cleanse/detox at least three to four times per year. The smoothies listed in this ebook should give you some idea and perhaps even help you to start a healthier life.

Smoothies And Weight Loss

In the United States of America obesity is rampant -- this is an indisputable fact. With regulations being passed on food servings and the weight of the average school child skyrocketing, the need for action has never been more dire. Obesity can lead to heart disease among other rather nasty conditions, and with that being the case, many are turning to more alternative diets including the Atkins and Mediterranean. The problems with these diets have been kindly pointed out by nutritionists for years, though none so much as the Atkins diet. With the Atkins diet you will completely forego the inclusion of carbohydrates within your diet, and while this will eventually cause you to lose weight, you will find that it can have other side effects as well. As a matter of fact, many people have actually died using the Atkins diet! That being said, it is important to find a diet that will meet your needs without causing you to drop dead at work or at school. This is where the Smoothie Diet will come into play.

Why would you be able to lose more weight with smoothies than other diets? Many of them taste downright outstanding, and as you know, you can't lose weight with something that tastes good. The truth however is that a smoothie will give you all of the necessary nutrients in a single glass without the unnecessary calories. As you learn more about smoothies and study the ingredients you will find that you can build a great combination that balances protein, healthy fats, vitamins, nutrients, and complex carbohydrates.

Yes, smoothies can be designed to help you lose weight, but you may also find it necessary to develop one that boost your metabolic rate.

This will of course involve providing you with more energy, and filling you up. Gaining energy in this manner will save you from needing to head to the store and grab one of those Five Hour Energy drinks. There is nothing quite like doing it naturally, and let's face it, Mother Nature has all the ingredients we require, and she is more than willing to cater to our needs if we just listen.

Benefits of Soy Milk

Throughout this e-Book you may see us refer to Soy Milk or Almond Milk quite a bit. There is a reason for this! Soy milk is much healthier than regular milk, being naturally high in essential fatty acids, proteins, fiber, vitamins, and of course, minerals. These are the nutrients your body needs to function at maximum capacity, though you might be wondering exactly what Soy Milk can do for you in the long run.

The first thing that people will notice(if they are paying attention) is the improvement of their lipid profile. Unlike dairy milk, soy milk does not feature the same saturated fat or cholesterol. Soy milk is typically unsaturated, features no cholesterol, and is actually capable of inhibiting the transport of cholesterol into your bloodstream using the monounsaturated and polyunsaturated fatty acids. Regular intake of soy can actually lower triglycerides and LDL, or low density lipoproteins. If you have a history of heart disease in your family, soy milk might be the answer for you. In any case, it is always the answer when it comes to a proper smoothie weight loss diet.

What about blood vessel integrity? This is just as vital when it comes to basic survival, and it is another reason that we tend to include soy milk so often in our recipes. Soy contains omega-3 and omega-6 fatty acids along with phyto-antioxidants that will serve to protect your blood vessels from hemorrhage. These will also protect your lining cells from free radical attacks as well as cholesterol deposits. This is yet another reason why smoothies will help you lose weight AND keep your body in top shape.

Finally we have weight loss. That's why we're here, right? Though most people don't realize it, milk actually contains sugar by itself. Cow's milk contains 12 grams of sugar per cup, though soy milk only contains 7 grams per cup. Because soy milk only has 80 calories, it is the equivalent of skim milk. Through drinking soy milk you will gain extra fiber, and ultimately feel full for a longer period of time.

In a Nutshell:

Less Sugar than Cow Milk
Supports Blood Vessel Integrity
No Cholesterol
Inhibits Transport of Cholesterol to Bloodstream
Lowers Triglycerides and LDL
Encourages Weight Loss

In the end soy milk might be a bit more expensive than regular milk, but it will help you to feel fuller for longer, and will eventually drive your food costs down. In addition to that you will feel much healthier in the coming weeks.

Part 1: Fruit Smoothies

Fruit smoothies are not necessarily a health smoothie, though they do help individuals to lose weight. These smoothies do a great job of creating a meal replacement diet, ultimately giving you a tasty treat whenever you need one! Fruit smoothies are great for breakfast or for a quick snack at any point during the day. The best part is the way they fill you up. Rather than empty calories, fruit smoothies provide all the nutrients you require to keep you full and keep your hand out of the cookie jar. Each fruit smoothie will obviously consist of a base, and many people choose to use a banana. Others will opt for various flavors of yogurt, and in the end, it is totally up to you. You have so many different choices for bases and flavors, so go over the following recipes and see which suits you best for your day to day meal replacement!

Recipe #1. The Basic Fruit Smoothie:

What we have here is the basic fruit smoothie containing all of the ingredients you need to embark on your own sensational adventure in taste. From strawberries to chunked banana, you have all the essential fruits and more if you feel like experimenting!

Items Needed:

Blender or Smoothie Maker
Glasses

Ingredients:

1 Quart Hulled Strawberries

1 Chunked Banana

2 Peaches Pitted and Chunked

2 Cups of Ice (Small Chunks)

1 Cup of Orange, Peach, or Mango Juice

Preparation Instructions:

Place all of the fruit in a large blender, use the high setting until fruit is pureed. Once this is accomplished, add in your choice of orange, peach, or mango juice and continue blending until you achieve the consistency you want. Once completed, you may pour into glasses garnish with a slice of fruit and serve.

Note: Because this is the basic smoothie, you may feel free to try different ingredient combinations for different taste experiences.

Recipe #2: The Frozen Banana Smoothie

Though this is a smoothie of the frozen banana variety, banana will not be used as the base. Instead, lowfat Vanilla Yogurt will be used along with an amount of orange juice. All of the ingredients are fairly soft, meaning you can use a basic blender rather than a smoothie maker or juicer. This is one of the easiest smoothies to make so long as you have all of the ingredients on hand or can get to them easily.

Items Needed:

Blender or Smoothie Maker
Glasses

Ingredients:

1 Cup of Sliced Strawberries
1 6 oz cup of Lowfat Vanilla Yogurt
2 Frozen Bananas
2/3 Cup of Pulp-Free Orange Juice

Preparation Instructions:

Place the fruit ingredients into the blender on high and blend until fruit is pureed. Add yogurt pulsing it just enough to start the mixing process. Next pour in the juice and blend on medium until you reach the desired thickness. Pour into your glasses and serve.

Recipe #3: The Banana Berry Colada

Though you might not live near a beach, there is no reason you shouldn't be able to enjoy a tropical drink here and there – even if you're on a diet. This recipe brings the tropical island feel to you, and gives you the taste you crave without the alcoholic aftertaste.

Items Needed:

Blender or Smoothie Maker
Glasses

Ingredients:

3 Cups of Small Cubed Ice
1/2 Cup of Frozen Strawberries
1 Cup Pina Colada Mix
2 Whole Frozen Bananas
1/2 Cup of Yogurt

Preparation Instructions:

Layer all the ingredients in your blender and blend on high for about 80 to 90 seconds. Serve immediately.

Note: If you cannot find strawberries(they occasionally go out of season) you can use strawberry syrup as a substitute.

Recipe #4: The Basic Grape Smoothie

For this recipe most people will actually recommend that you use red grapes, though to be perfectly honest you can use anything you want. Keep in mind that the ingredients mentioned make for a great smoothie, but you can replace the skim milk with regular milk, or the plain yogurt with low fat yogurt. Feel free to experiment and come up with the perfect combination for your needs.

Items Needed:

Blender or Smoothie Maker
Glasses

Ingredients:

2 Cups of Seedless Grapes of any color
1 Cup of Skim Milk
2 Tablespoons of Sugar
1 Cup of Plain Yogurt

Preparation Instructions:

Place grapes and sugar into the blender on medium and mix thoroughly. Add in the yogurt and blend for another 10 seconds on medium. Pour in the milk and blend on high. Proceed with this until the mixture is perfectly smooth.

Note: Though you are free to use any type of grape for this smoothie, it is recommended that you purchase a bushel of seedless grapes to avoid not having enough for everyone.

Recipe #5: Raspberry-Orange Smoothie

Orange is in fashion with this smoothie, but before you embark on this journey of taste, make sure you are actually using pulp free orange juice. In addition to that, you should of course make sure you are using ice cubes rather than chipped ice or straight water. The last thing you want to do is water down a tasty smoothie!

Items Needed:

Blender or Smoothie Maker
Glasses

Ingredients:

1 Cup Pulp Free Orange Juice
1 Cup of Raspberries
1/2 Cup of Plain Yogurt
2 Cup Sugar
1 Cup of Small Cube Ice
1 Sprig of Mint for garnish

Preparation Instructions:

Place your orange juice, raspberries, and sugar into your blender, mix on medium for 60 seconds. Add in the yogurt and blend for another 30 seconds. Toss in your ice and blend on high until you have the thickness desired. Pour into your glasses, garnish with a sprig of mint and serve.

Recipe #6: Kiwi-Apple Smoothie

If you're ready for something tasty then you've come to the right place. This mixture of fruits and vegetables might as well be a taste of heaven, and the best part is you can choose which leafy greens you want to include in your new concoction. Then again, you are free to experiment and remove the greens entirely! Remember – the smoothie is your oyster!

Items Needed:

Blender or Smoothie Maker
Glasses

Ingredients:

2 Kiwi Fruit Peeled
2 Apples Peeled and Cored
2 Cups Leafy Greens
1 Full Size Carrot
1/2 Cup of Water

Preparation Instructions:

Place the carrots and apples into the blender, pulse until small enough pieces to place the blender on high for another 60 seconds. Put in the leafy greens and water, blend on high for 30 seconds. Then add in the kiwis. Blend again on high until your desired thickness. Garnish with a slice of kiwi fruit if desired and serve.

Note: The leafy green may be lettuce or spinach. Baby spinach is recommended.

Recipe #7: Apple-Lemon Smoothie

Are you ready to try something sweet and sour? You've come to the right page! For this one all you need are a few ingredients and a bit of imagination. It's time to give your taste buds an experience that they will never forget, at least until you drink your next cup of hot coffee.

Items Needed:

Blender or Smoothie Maker
Glasses

Ingredients:

2 Apples (Any variety)
1 Full Sized Carrot
1/2 Cup of Water
2 Cups of Leafy Greens

Preparation Instructions:

Clean and peel your carrot, leaving one peel for garnish. Then slice the remaining it into small chunks. Core and cube your apples. Toss your carrots it into the blender. Pulse a few times and then add in the apples and water. Keep pulsing until partially smooth. Add in your leafy greens, and put the blender on high until the desired consistency is reached. Pour into a glass and garnish with a strip of carrot on top.

Note: The leafy green may be lettuce or spinach. Baby spinach is recommended. It is also important to remember that apple skin must be left intact. While the apple should be ripe, it should not be brown on the interior or close to rotten. The skin of the apple contains plenty of nutrients and will help contribute to a healthy diet. That being said, choose your apples carefully and make sure you are using the same two apples in your smoothie. For example if you use a Gala apple, use two Galas, or if you use a Red Delicious, make sure the other is Red Delicious as well. The result will be a delicious meal replacement snack!

Recipe #8: Pear-Nut Smoothie

This recipe, unlike some of the others we have mentioned previously actually uses water as a base rather than yogurt or banana, even though banana is used as a core ingredient in this recipe. Keep in mind that you are using a peeled, frozen banana in this recipe, so it might be a good idea to invest in a high end blender or a smoothie maker not only to ensure that there is no damage to the device, but also to ensure that you achieve a perfect mixture. In addition to that, it may be helpful to acquire a glass blender container as these tend to be tougher.

Items Needed:

Blender or Smoothie Maker
Glasses

Ingredients:

1 Frozen and Peeled Banana
1/4 Cup Raw nuts
2 pears cored
1/2 Cup of Water
12 Ice Cubes

Preparation Instructions:

Pour water into your blender. Start layering your ingredients with the nuts on bottom, pears and ice in the middle and the bananas on top. Blend on low speed for 20 seconds. Increase to high speed until drink becomes smooth.

Recipe #9: Nutty Creamy Apple Smoothie

If you're not allergic to nuts then you might find this smoothie agreeable to your pallet. If you are, then you can always remove the nuts. Keep in mind that this recipe uses both water and yogurt as the base, making it a rather unique concoction. If you find that you do not like the consistency, you are always free to change it and experiment with different mixtures.

Items Needed:

Blender or Smoothie Maker
Glasses

Ingredients:

1 Banana, Peeled/Frozen
1/4 Cup Raw nuts
2 apples cored
1/2 Cup of Water
6 oz Plain Yogurt
12 Ice Cubes

Preparation Instructions:

Pour water into blender, layer the ingredients with the nuts on the bottom, apples and ice in the middle and the banana and yogurt on top. Blend on low speed for 20 seconds. Increase to high speed until drink becomes smooth.

Recipe #10: Apple-Blueberry Smoothie

Apple and Blueberry are not typically seen together outside of a pancake or waffle setting, but they make fro a great smoothie along with avocado and leafy greens. You would do well to give this smoothie a try and augment your diet!

Items Needed:

Blender or Smoothie Maker
Glasses

Ingredients:

1 Cup of Blueberries
1 Apple
2 Cups of Leafy Greens
¼ Cup of Avocado
½ Cup of Water

Preparation Instructions:

Peel and remove the pit on the avocado then remove the core on the apple and cube bothe fruits. Pour the water into the blender, then toss in your apple. Pulse a few times to help break it down then add in the rest of your ingredients. Blend on medium for 30 seconds, then on high until you reach the desired consistency. Pour into your glass and top with one whole blueberry then serve.

Recipe #11: Cherry Apple Smoothie

Cherries and apples are always going to be popular. After all, they taste pretty great, don't they? This smoothie combines the two along with leafy greens, though as always, you may feel free to remove the leafy greens and make it exclusively fruit.

Items Needed:

Blender or Smoothie Maker
Glasses

Ingredients:

1 Cup cherries
1 Whole apple
2 Cups of fresh Leafy Green
½ Cup of Pure Water

Preparation Instructions:

Remove the stems and seeds from the cherries. Then core and cube your apple. In your blender add in your water and apple. Pulse these two items together for 30 seconds. Next add in the rest of your ingredients and blend on high until the smoothie is of the desired thickness. Pour into a glass and serve.

Recipe #12: CranBananaSmoothie

Though this smoothie might be filled with leafy greens, it is still not considered a green smoothie. By adding ½ cup of cranberries and a banana, we are creating what might be one of the healthiest and tastiest smoothies out there. That being said, you will most certainly want to put this one to the test as soon as you get the chance. Be warned that this DOES use water as a base, and therefore might not be quite as thick as most would prefer.

Items Needed:

Blender or Smoothie Maker
Glasses

Ingredients:

1/2 cup cranberries
1 Banana
2 cups fresh Leafy Greens
1 stalk of organic celery
3 Dates for Sweetening Purposes
4-6 Ounces of Water

Preparation Instructions:

Place the celery and water into your blender pulse 10 times to start breaking it down. Then add in the leafy greens, pulsing another 10 times. Toss in all of the fruit and blend on medium until desired consistency is achieved. Pour into your glass and enjoy.

Recipe #13: Plum-Apple-LemonSmoothie

This is another recipe that uses water as a base, but there is nothing quite like a good plum. These fruits have an entirely different taste, and make an outstanding addition to any smoothie. Combined with lemon juice and apple, you know your taste buds are in for the ultimate treat.

Items Needed:

Blender or Smoothie Maker
Glasses

Ingredients:

1 Plum Deseeded
1 Apple Cored
½ Lemon juiced
2 Cups of fresh Baby Spinach
1 Medium Carrot, Chopped
1/2 cup water

Preparation Instructions:

Place the water and chopped carrot into the blender use pulse a few times to help to break down the carrot. Add in the apple and pulse another 10 times. Layer in the last of the ingredients and starting on low speed work your way up to high until smooth. Pour into a glass and enjoy.

Recipe #14: Plum-Banana Smoothie

Because this recipe does not actually call for a frozen banana, you can use one at room temperature, and you will be able to use a blender rather than a smoothie maker. As always, try to ensure that all of the fruit is deseeded and preferably ripened.

Items Needed:

Blender or Smoothie Maker
Glasses

Ingredients:

2 plums, deseeded
1 banana, peeled
2 cups fresh baby spinach (or other leafy green)
½ vine ripe tomato
1/2 – 1 cup water

Preparation Instructions:

Pour the water into the blender with the plumbs and tomato. Blend on the low setting for 30 seconds. Then add in the leafy greens and banana blending on high until well blended and you reach the thickness desired.

Recipe #15: Kiwi-Banana Smoothie

This is yet another recipe that makes use of bananas, though we also have kiwis in the mixture. It is important to ensure you have enough kiwis if you choose to use the baby variant. Ideally you would obtain full grown kiwis, but sometimes the store simply does not have them. Try to remember this when you are picking up your ingredients! Because the kiwi fruit will typically be peeled, it should not be too tough on your blender.

Items Needed:

Blender or Smoothie Maker
Glasses

Ingredients:

2 kiwi fruit
1 banana
2 cups fresh baby spinach (or other leafy green)
¼ avocado
1/2 cup water

Preparation Instructions:

Peel your kiwi fruit and banana. Peel and remove the pit from your avocado. Layer all ingredients into your blender. Blend on high for at least 60 seconds. You may need longer to reach the desired consistency.

Recipe #16: Kiwi-Mint Smoothie

Who doesn't like the taste of mint? Mint is used in all sort of tasty snacks, and often combined with chocolate. In this case however, mint is being combined with kiwi, banana, and spinach leaves if you so desire. Keep in mind that you can always swap the spinach for another leafy green, or remove it completely if that sounds more desirable. This smoothie is in your hands, and in your blender.

Items Needed:

Blender or Smoothie Maker
Glasses

Ingredients:

2 kiwi fruit
1 banana
2 cups fresh baby spinach (or other leafy green)
4 mint leaves
1/2 cup water

Preparation Instructions:

Peel your kiwi fruit and banana, slicing them up. Save a half of a slice of kiwi fruit for garnish. Layer all ingredients in the blender, and blend on high until smooth. Pour... Serve... Enjoy...

Recipe #17: Cantaloupe Strawberry Smoothie

This is yet another recipe that might not be for everyone, but it does provide a slightly different taste if you are tired of the same routine over and over again. Once again you may feel free to leave the spinach out if you feel like going full fruit.

Items Needed:

Blender
Glasses

Ingredients:

1/2 medium/large cantaloupe
1 cup organic strawberries
2 cups fresh organic baby spinach (or other leafy green)
1/4 cup filtered water if needed

Preparation Instructions:

Cut your cantaloupe in half, scooping out all of the seeds. Slice it into manageable sizes and then make cubes while still on the rind. Cut the cantaloupe from the rind. Remove the hull from your strawberries and the stems from your leafy greens if needed. Place all ingredients into the blender, and blend on high for about 60 seconds. Add the water and blend for another 30 seconds if needed for desired thickness.

Recipe #18: Cantaloupe-Apple Smoothie

When you're in the mood for something a little different, why not going the cantaloupe-apple route? This is an organic recipe and is highly recommended for those who are attempting to lose weight. As always, we recommend this smoothie for those who are seeking something a bit lighter than those typically made from yogurt.

Items Needed:

Blender or Smoothie Maker
Glasses

Ingredients:

– 1/2 medium/large cantaloupe
– 1 organic apple with skin
– 2 cups fresh organic baby spinach (or other leafy green)
– 1/4 cup filtered water if needed

Preparation Instructions:

Cut your cantaloupe in half, scooping out all of the seeds. Slice it into manageable sizes and then make cubes while still on the rind. Cut the cantaloupe from the rind. Core your apple and cube it as well. Place your apples in your blender and pulse 10 times so that they are starting to get smooth. Add in the cantaloupe and baby spinach. Blend on medium for 30 seconds, then add water if needed to help to smooth out your drink. Blend on high for another 30 seconds or more to get the consistency you desire.

Recipe #19: Pumpkin-Apple Smoothie w/ Cinnamon

Anyone who says pumpkins are only for Halloween has never bought one out of season and turned it into an epic smoothie. If you cannot find pumpkins in your area, you have the option of finding cooked or canned pumpkin at your local grocery store. Nothing tastes quite as good as the real thing of course, but with a smoothie like this, you may have to settle for 'as close as possible'. In spite of that, this is an amazing concoction that you simply will not want to miss!

Items Needed:

Blender
Glasses

Ingredients:

– 1 cup pumpkin (cooked, canned, or raw)
– 1 apple
– 1 banana
– dash of cinnamon (to taste)
– 2 cups or handfuls fresh baby spinach (optional, but recommended)
– 4-6 ounces of fresh water or pumpkin seed milk (or try coconut water)

Preparation Instructions:

Prepare your pumpkin if needed. Core and cube the apple, place in the blender with your liquid and pulse a few times to break it down. Peel your banana, then add it and the other ingredients to the blender. Blending on medium for 30 seconds, moving up to high until you reach the desired consistency. Pour, garnish, and serve.

Recipe #20: Basic Sweet Grapefruit

While most people do not associate the words 'grapefruit' and 'sweet', here we have an outstanding grapefruit smoothie that simply requires water and a banana for the base. As always the leafy greens are optional, unless of course you're in a spinach type of mood.

Items Needed:

Blender or Smoothie Maker
Glasses

Ingredients:

1 grapefruit
1 banana
2 cups fresh baby spinach (or other leafy green)
4 ounces of water

Preparation Instructions:

Peel your banana and grapefruit. Remove all seeds from the grapefruit. Layer your ingredients with the leafy greens on the bottom and the banana on top. Pour the water on top and blend on high for 60 seconds or longer to reach the desired consistency.

Recipe #21: Watermelon-Banana Smoothie

Like several other fruits we have mentioned in this article, watermelon are typically seasonal, though they are grown constantly in the more weather permitting parts of the world. When you are making your watermelon smoothie, it would be within your best interest to remove all the seeds, or purchase a seedless watermelon.

Items Needed:

Blender
Glasses

Ingredients:

2 cups seedless watermelon
1 whole banana
2 cups fresh baby spinach (or other leafy green)
1/2 cup water if needed

Preparation Instructions:

Place your leafy greens in your blender and press pulse 3 times to help to break down the fibers quickly. Place the remaining ingredients in the blend and blend on high for another 60 seconds. If you want the smoothie less thick add in the water and blend for another 30 to 60 seconds.

Recipe #22: Watermelon-Pear Smoothie

Once again we're dealing with a seedless watermelon(unless you want to use one of the seeded variety and pick the seeds out by yourself), and this time it is mixed with a pear! As you may already know, the pear happens to be one of the most incredible fruits on the face of the planet, and one that will need to be cored before use. The pear is a fairly soft fruit, and this means your smoothie will be ready within a matter of minutes. You may feel free to use either a smoothie maker or a blender for this endeavor.

Items Needed:

Blender or Smoothie Maker
Glasses

Ingredients:

2 cups seedless watermelon
1 pear
2 cups fresh baby spinach (or other leafy green)
½ cup water if needed

Preparation Instructions:

Remove the core and seeds on your pear. Place it and the leafy greens into the blender. Pulse 10 times, then add in your watermelon and blend on high for 60 seconds. Add water if needed to reach the desired consistency and blend for an additional 3 seconds. Serve and enjoy.

Recipe #23: Tangerine-Coconut Smoothie

If you're ready to move into the more exotic portion of the menu, then it's time to have a look at this amazing tangerine coconut concoction. As with all the other it stars a banana, but it also involves an amount of cocounut water. This is one fruit smoothie that you simply will not want to miss!

Items Needed:

Blender
Glasses

Ingredients:

2 tangerines, peeled and deseeded
1 young green or Thai coconut (meat)
1 banana (or 2 cups papaya, cubed)
2 cups fresh baby spinach (or other leafy green)
2 celery stalks (optional)
4-6 ounces of coconut water

Preparation Instructions:

Place the celery in the blender and pulse to start breaking it down. Place the tangerines in next and blend that on slow for another 30 seconds. Add in the last of the ingredients and blend them in for another 60 seconds. Serve and enjoy.

Recipe #24: Tangerine-Pineapple Smoothie

We've mentioned a lot of different great mixtures, but none quite as fun as the tangerine smoothie. When combined with pineapple, you will rather easily see that this is one of the greatest and healthiest smoothies in the fruit section. If you wish, you can replace the banana in this recipe with two cubes of papaya.

Items Needed:

Blender or Smoothie Maker
Glasses

Ingredients:

2 tangerines
2 cups pineapple
1 banana
2 stalks of celery
2 cups fresh baby spinach (or other leafy green)
4-6 ounces of water or tangerine juice

Preparation Instructions:

Place your celery in your blender and use pulse until everything is broken down. Peel and remove the seeds from your tangerine, add it into the blender using pulse a few more times. Add in the remainder of the ingredients and blend on high until everything is smooth and still thick.

Recipe #25: Pineapple-Vanilla Smoothie

For the first time we are going to discuss a vanilla smoothie, and vanilla does far more than simply add flavor. There are many studies proving that the scent of vanilla alone could assist those who are seeking to better themselves by losing weight. Naturally the details are still being investigated, and those who do take advantage of it will still nee to get plenty of exercise. In spite of this, it is still a great weight loss supplement and something to keep in mind when you start dieting.

Another respectable property of vanilla is the way that it manages to reduce both stress and anxiety. A number of studies have shown it relives these conditions which has quite a bit to do with the scent. It has long been recommended that those suffering from stress or anxiety simply sip water or milk mixed with a bit of vanilla extract. Not only would this help to get rid of the stress, but also other problems that may or may not be related to the stress your body is experiencing.

Items Needed:

Blender
Glasses

Ingredients:

1 cup pineapple
1 banana
1/2 vanilla bean (or more to add extra taste)
2 cups fresh baby spinach (or other leafy green)
1 celery stalk
1/2 – 1 cup water

Preparation Instructions:

Scrape the inside of the vanilla bean, and place what you have in the blender. Toss in your celery and pulse 30 times or until the celery is broken down. Then add in the pineapple pulsing another 3 times to start breaking it down. Add in the remaining ingredients, and blend on medium for another 60 seconds until you reach the consistency desired. Pour, garnish, and enjoy.

Part 2: Green Smoothies

What is the green smoothie exactly? How does it work? Why does it work? Why should you incorporate it into your everyday life? Believe it or not, many people are now taking part in the tradition we rather fondly refer to as the green smoothie with good reason. After all, more than a few people have lost up to 40 pounds, and some have actually managed to relive themselves of serious health problems simply by drinking a green smoothie every day as part of their meal plan. Before we discuss some of the better green smoothie recipes, let's talk about the health benefits that you are certain to encounter.

If you really want to lose weight, then you really need to make use of the green smoothie solution. These smoothies, like the others, will provide plenty of nutrition, minerals, vitamins, fiber, and of course healthy carbohydrates. These will all contribute to your eventual weight loss of course, and they will even help you to reduce your hunger pangs. At some point, most people experience fewer cravings for junk food and more cravings for healthy alternatives.

With that being said, it is no surprise that eating a smoothie every single day will often end with an individual craving healthy foods, and will also result in them eating the recommended 5-9 services of fruit and vegetables each day. Keep in mind that the more fruits and vegetables you eat, the better chance you will stand of fighting cancer and other diseases. The greatest benefit of the green smoothie of course is the inclusion of fruit which serves to mask the taste of vegetables. This makes it very easy to consume the allotted amount and give you the healthy advantage you need.

While eating your fruits and vegetables is always recommended, it can be somewhat hard to digest them alone. By blending these ingredients you will bread down the cells of the plants and render them much easier to digest. The blender will actually maximize the delivery of nutrients to your body, and it is much more convenient than preparing a salad. When you are on the go, there is nothing quite as efficient as drinking your meal through a straw.

It is no surprise that green smoothies will be high in antioxidants as well as phytonutrients. This gives your body a great way to protect itself against disease, and a great way to boost your energy. These are natural, whole foods that will give you the energy you need to get through your day.

Why not simply drink juice or use a juicer rather than drinking smoothies all the time? The benefit of a smoothie, of course, is that your drink will use the whole fruit and vegetable. These are not processed or littered with preservatives. Instead, you have a drink that is high in both fiber and nutrition. If you want to increase your colon health and your health overall, this is the solution you've been looking for.

Once you take full advantage of the green smoothies, especially the ones we will mention in the next section, you will find that you even gain a clearer, more radiant exterior. Because smoothies are high in fiber, they eliminate toxins properly. This is yet another reason that smoothies are outstanding when it comes to cleansing the body. To reduce your craving for junk food and give yourself a great advantage, start looking over the available smoothie recipes and use them to your advantage!

Recipe #1: Banana-Papaya Smoothie

It's time to take a look at one of our simpler smoothies, which happens to be the Banana-Papaya. With just four ingredients and a lot of taste, you stand a great chance of cleansing your body and getting the daily energy you need.

Items Needed:

Blender or Smoothie Maker
Glasses

Ingredients:

1 Banana
1 Papaya
2 leaves Swiss Chard
2 cups water

Preparation Instructions:

Put your Swiss Chard into the blender and pulse 5 times to start breaking it down. Add in your papaya and blend on low for 30 seconds. Add in the banana and water, blend on high for another 60 seconds. Pour, garnish, serve, and enjoy.

Recipe #2: Dandelion Smoothie

It might sound a bit strange to some, but Dandelions tend to make some of the best smoothies, even if the color isn't actually green.

Items Needed:

Blender
Glasses

Ingredients:

Handful of Organic Dandelions
1 Banana
1 Pear
1 Mango
2 cups water

Preparation Instructions:

Peel the banana and mango, slicing both up. Remove the core and seeds from the pear. Toss the dandelions into the blender pulsing 3 times. Then add in the mango and pear pulsing an additional 10 times. Last place in the last few ingredients and blend on high for a final 60 seconds or until you reach the consistency desired. Pour, garnish, serve, and enjoy.

Recipe #3: Romaine Lettuce and Avocado Smoothie

For this one you are most definitely going to want a good blender, though the ingredients are not bound to be too harsh on the machine. The recipe uses water as a base, as most green smoothies tend to do.

Items Needed:

Blender
Glasses

Ingredients:

3 leaves of Romaine Lettuce
½ an Avocado
½ Fuji Apple
1 Banana
2 cups water

Preparation Instructions:

Make sure to blend the romaine lettuce before inserting the other ingredients. Once blended, proceed to do the same with the other ingredients for approximately 60 seconds. Pour, garnish, serve, and enjoy.

Recipe #4: Fuji-Apple Avocado Smoothie

The Fuji Apple is not something that you will find in nature – usually. Instead, ti is actually a fruit developed at a Tohoku research station in Japan. It was first brought to the market in 1962, and since then has been filling stomachs and serving as a staple in smoothies all over the world.

Items Needed:

Blender
Glasses

Ingredients:

5 leaves Purple Kale
½ Orange
½ Fuji Apple
Small piece of Ginger
½ an Avocado

Preparation Instructions:

Place all ingredients apart from the apple into your blender, pulse for 30 seconds. Place the apple inside and then pulse for another 30. Check to ensure the mixture is completed, then proceed to drink, or continue blending if not complete.

Recipe #5: Rainbow-Chard Smoothie

If you were looking for the ultimate in health drinks then congratulations, here it is. The rainbow-chard smoothie is obviously based on chard, a vegetable typically used in Mediterranean cooking. Chard leaves are usually green, but in the case of rainbow chard, the stalk is a different color. Chard is thought to be one of the healthiest vegetables in the world, having extremely nutritious leaves, and always available when you want to make something.

Items Needed:

Blender
Glasses

Ingredients:

1 cup frozen Strawberries
1 Banana
1 Mango
2 cups water
2 leaves Rainbow Chard

Preparation Instructions:

Peel the banana and mango, slicing them both up into smaller bits. Now you will want to layer the ingredients from hardest on the bottom to softest on the top. You will want your rainbow chard closer to the bottom to help break up the fibers. Top with the water and blend on high until you have reached the desired consistency.

Recipe #6: Spinach-Banana Smoothie

This is the ultimate in green smoothie recipes. It might not give you the ability to leap tall buildings or show off muscles on par with Popeye, but ti will keep you quite healthy, and it will give you something to talk about!

Items Needed:

Blender(or Smoothie Maker)
Glasses

Ingredients:
1 large handful of Spinach
1 Banana
1 cup frozen Strawberries
1 Orange
Small piece of Ginger
2 cups water

Preparation Instructions:

Peel your banana, and slice it up. Peel your ginger if not already done and grate that into the blender. Next put the spinach in the blender with the frozen strawberries and pulse 10 times. Add the last of the ingredients and blend on high until you reach the desired consistency.

Recipe #7: Young Coconut-Pineapple Smoothie

This recipe is not intended to serve quite as many as the others, but if you want to scale it up a bit, make sure you replace the ingredients listed with either larger quantities or larger items. Before doing so, keep in mind that by using a young coconut you will gain more Vitamin B6, niacin, and folic acid.

Items Needed:

Blender(or Smoothie Maker)
Glasses

Ingredients:

1 young Coconut
½ of a small Pineapple
½ Pear
5 Leaves of Romaine Lettuce

Preparation Instructions:

Remove the meat from the coconut, and put it off to the side. Remove the pineapple from the rind and slice that up into chunks. Remove the core and seeds on your pear, cubing that half right into the blender. Pulse these together 5 times. Add in the remainder of the ingredients into the blender and blend on medium until the desired consistency is reached.

Recipe #8: Red Lettuce and Raspberry Smoothie

Items Needed:

Blender(or Smoothie Maker)
Glasses

Ingredients:

1 cup frozen Raspberries
5 leaves Red Leaf Lettuce
1 Red Apple
1 Green Apple
½ of a small Pineapple
2 cups water

Preparation Instructions:

Remove the ride on your pineapple, and cube up the half that you need. Remove the core and the seeds from your apples also cubing them. Toss your frozen fruit and apples into your blender pulsing 10 times to start breaking them down. add in the lettuce and and blend on low for 15 seconds, then add in the pineapple and water blending an additional 60 seconds on medium or until you reach the desired consistency.

Recipe #9: Bell Pepper-Avocado Smoothie

Items Needed:

Blender(or Smoothie Maker)
Glasses

Ingredients:

1 large handful of Spinach
¾ of Orange Bell Pepper
½ an Avocado
3 cloves Garlic
2 Tomatoes
2 cups of water

Preparation Instructions:

Peel and grate your cloves of garlic directly into the blender. Slice up the
bell pepper and remove the seeds. Cube the portion you are using into
the blender. Peel the half of avocado and cube it up into the blender as
well. Add in your spinach and then cut your tomatoes in half tossing
them seeds and all into the blender. Top with the water then blend on
high for 2 minutes or until you reach the desired consistency.

Recipe #10: Tomatocado

Items Needed:

Blender(or Smoothie Maker)
Glasses

Ingredients:

½ an Avocado
2 Tomatoes
Pinch of Cayenne Pepper
Pinch of Salt
½ of a Red Onion
1 Orange Bell Pepper
2 cups water

Preparation Instructions:

peel the half of avocado, and cube it into a bowl. Slice the tomatoes into quarters, and place those in the bowl with the avocado. Peel the onion and slice chunks into your blender. Cut the peper in half and remove the seeds, toss your slices into the blender as well. Place the water and seasoning into the blender. Pulse these together 10 times. Then add your moist ingredients and blend on medium until the desired consistency is reached.

Recipe #11: Red 'n Green

Items Needed:

Blender(or Smoothie Maker)
Glasses

Ingredients:

2 Bananas
3 pieces of Celery
1 head of Red Leaf Lettuce
2 cups water

Preparation Instructions:

Chop the celery up into chunks placing them into the blender. Slice the lettuce up into manageable chunks tossing them into the blender one at a time pulsing 5 times between each chunk. Once the lettuce is broken down some, add in the water and peeled banana. Blend on high for 2 minutes or until the desired consistency is reached.

Recipe #12: Celery-Banana Smoothie

Items Needed:

Blender(or Smoothie Maker)
Glasses

Ingredients:

2 Bananas
3 Pieces of Celery
1 Head of Red Leaf Lettuce
2 cups water

Preparation Instructions:

chunk the celery into the blender and pulse 10 times to start breaking it
down. Add in the water and lettuce, blending on low for 20 seconds.
Add in the bananas and blend on high until the desired consistency is
reached.

Recipe #13: Kale-Banana Smoothie

Items Needed:

Blender(or Smoothie Maker)
Glasses

Ingredients:

2 Leaves Purple Kale
2 Leaves Collard Greens
2 Bananas
½ an Asian Pear
2 Cups water
1 Cup frozen Raspberries

Preparation Instructions:

Slice the pear in half and remove the seeds and core. Chunk it up into the blender adding the frozen raspberries and pulse 10 times. add the kale and collard greens, blending for 30 seconds on low. Add the water and bananas blending on high until the desired consistency is reached.

Recipe #14: Blueberry-Spinach Smoothie

Items Needed:

Blender(or Smoothie Maker)
Glasses

Ingredients:

1 cup frozen Blueberries
¼ pound Spinach
1 Orange
1 cup water

Preparation Instructions:

Peel your orange and remove all the seeds. Place the orange slices into the blender adding the frozen blueberries. Blend on low for 20 seconds. Add the spinach and water then blend on high until you reach the desired consistency.

Recipe #15: Lovely Tomato

Items Needed:

Blender(or Smoothie Maker)
Glasses

Ingredients:

4 Tomatoes
1 Red Bell Pepper
1 bunch Basil
½ an Avocado

Preparation Instructions:

Slice your pepper in half and remove the seeds. Cut it into strips into your blender. Slice your tomatoes in half over the blender tossing them in when done. Add in the basil and blend on low for 60 seconds. While that is blending, peel your avocado and cube it, placing the pieces into the blender. After the last ingredients are in the blender place it on high until the desired consistency is reached.

Recipe #16: Purple Rainbow

Items Needed:

Blender(or Smoothie Maker)
Glasses

Ingredients:

4 leaves Collard Greens
4 leaves Purple Kale
2 Leaves Rainbow Chard
1 Asian Pear
Piece of Ginger
1 Banana
1 cup frozen Blueberries
2 cups water.

Preparation Instructions:

Slice your pear in half, remove the core and seeds, then cube the pear. Add the water, frozen blueberries and pear into your blender on high for 30 seconds. Peel and grate the ginger into the blender. Add the chard, kale and greens and blend on high for another 60 seconds or until the desired consistency is reached.

Recipe #17: The Monster

Items Needed:

Blender(or Smoothie Maker)
Glasses

Ingredients:

1 banana, chunked
1 cup chopped frozen pineapple
1 pear, coarsely chopped
1 cup orange juice
3 cups baby spinach leaves
1 tbsp. honey
3 tbsp. ground flaxseed

Preparation Instructions:

Place ingredients in a blender, food processor, or smoothie maker. Puree until smooth. If mixture is not sweet enough, feel free to add more honey. When you are satisfied, serve.

Recipe #18: Basic Green Smoothie

Items Needed:

Blender(or Smoothie Maker)
Glasses

Ingredients:

1 Banana(Frozen)
3 Handfuls of spinach
2 tablespoons peanut butter
2 tablespoons cocoa powder
1 to 1-1/2 cups almond milk

Preparation Instructions:

Peel the banana and cut it into chunks. Place it at the bottom of the blender with the spinach. put the peanut butter and cocoa powder in next. Pulse these together 10 times. Then pour in the almond milk and blend on high until the desired thickness is reached.

Recipe #19: Green Grape Smoothie

Items Needed:

Blender(or Smoothie Maker)
Glasses

Ingredients:

2 Cups Red Seedless Grapes
1 Cup Packed Greens- I used lettuce but Kale and Spinach are even
better
1 Medium Pear
1/2 Cup Frozen Pumpkin Pureé
2 Tbsp. Avocado
3/4 Cup Coconut Water
Optional: Ice Cubes

Preparation Instructions:

Cut the pear in half and remove the core and seeds then chop it into
rough cubes. Remove the skin from the avocado and place that in
blender with the pear and the greens. Blend on low for 30 seconds, add
remaining ingredients and blend on high for 60 seconds or until the
desired thickness.

Recipe #20: Pomegranate-Blueberry

Items Needed:

Blender(or Smoothie Maker)
Glasses

Ingredients:

1/4 cup fresh pomegranate juice or arils
1 oz (2 tablespoons) whole acai berry juice or 100 grams of frozenacai berry puree*
2 cups frozen wild blueberries
2 organic bananas
4 ounces filtered water (optional if needed)

Preparation Instructions:

Peel the bananas and cut them into rough chunks. Place all fruit into the blender and pulse 10 times to start breaking it down. Then add your liquids and blend on medium for 30 seconds. Turn to high until the desired thickness is reached.

Recipe #21: Acai Special

Items Needed:

Blender(or Smoothie Maker)
Glasses

Ingredients:

1 3.5 ounce serving of frozen acai puree
1 to 2 sprigs of fresh mint (to taste)
2 bananas
1 cup organic red grapes
1 small head of organic romaine lettuce
2 ounces filtered water

Preparation Instructions:

Peel your bananas and cut into rough chunks. Place the lettuce in the blender with the water and pulse 10 times to start breaking it down. Add the grapes, mint and banana blend on high for 30 seconds. Add the frozen acai puree and blend on high for another 30 seconds, or until desired thickness is reached.

Recipe #22: Cucumber-Pear

Items Needed:

Blender(or Smoothie Maker)
Glasses

Ingredients:

1 English Cucumber (or seedless)
2 pears
2 cups fresh baby spinach (or other leafy green)
1/2 cup of water

Preparation Instructions:

Remove the core and seeds from the pear then cut it into rough chunks. Place it in the blender with the water and spinach. Pulse 10 times to start breaking them down. Then peel the cucumber and cut it also into rough chunks. Place that into the blender and blend on high until the desired thickness is reached.

Recipe #23: Citrus Sweet Potato Smoothie

Items Needed:

Blender(or Smoothie Maker)
Glasses

Ingredients:
1 cup cooked and cooled sweet potato
2 oranges
1/4 teaspoon cinnamon

Preparation Instructions:

Remove the skins from the sweet potato while still warm but not hot.
Let finish cooling. If you want them to cool faster, you can cube them
now too. While they are cooling, peel your oranges and remove the
seeds. Once the sweet potato is ready, place it in the blender with the
orange and cinnamon. Bend on high until you have the desired
thickness.

Recipe #24: Banana and Broccoli Smoothie

Items Needed:

Blender(or Smoothie Maker)
Glasses

Ingredients:
2 large bananas
2 cups frozen broccoli, chopped
4 ounces of filtered water

Preparation Instructions:

Place the broccoli into the blender with the water and blend on low while you are peeling the bananas. Stop the blender and drop in the bananas and blend on medium for 60 seconds. If not smooth put on high until desired consistency is achieved.

Recipe #25: Celery-Red Grape Smoothie

Items Needed:

Blender(or Smoothie Maker)
Glasses

Ingredients:

1 cup red grapes
1 small banana
2 medium stalk of celery
2 ounces of filtered water if needed

Preparation Instructions:

Chop the celery into 1 inch chunks, place them in the blender with the grapes. pulse 10 times then put on low while you are peeling and chunking your banana. Toss the banana into the blender with everything else and add the water at this time if you like. Blend on high until you reach the consistency desired.

Recipe #26: Mango-Tomato Smoothie

Items Needed:

Blender(or Smoothie Maker)
Glasses

Ingredients:

1 Mango, peeled and pitted
4 Ounces almond or soy milk
2 Campari tomatoes
1 Cup pineapple
1 Cup cilantro
3 Cups fresh baby spinach

Preparation Instructions:

Peel and pit your mango, ensuring that it is properly sliced. Chop your tomatoes, pineapple, and baby spinach. Once these things are done you may place your ingredients in the blender, mix, and serve.

Part 3: Breakfast Smoothies

Recipe #1: Blueberry Banana

No matter who you are or how old you get, you always have time for a meal, or a meal replacement that involves blueberries and bananas!

Items Needed:

Blender(or Smoothie Maker)
Glasses

Ingredients:
1 cup frozen blueberries
1 banana
6 ounces plain nonfat plain yogurt
3/4 cup unsweetened almond milk
1 tablespoon ground flax seeds
1/2 cup ice cubes

Preparation Instructions:

Place ingredients in the blender and begin blending on low speed. Increase speed gradually until ingredients are smooth. Serve and drink.

Recipe #2: Oatmeal-Strawberry Smoothie

If you're a fan of strawberries or oatmeal, this is the perfect smoothie to meet the morning with. By adding a little bit of honey, was can enhance what might have otherwise been a rather dull breakfast!

Items Needed:

Blender(or Smoothie Maker)
Glasses

Ingredients:
3/4 cup soy milk
1/4 cup rolled oats
8 strawberries
1/4 teaspoon vanilla extract
1/2 banana
1 teaspoon honey

Preparation Instructions:

Blend all ingredients in a blender with a glass container, serve immediately, or later if you plan to cool them for a while.

Recipe #3: Basic Berry Smoothie

There is always plenty of reason to get back to the basics, and that is precisely what this smoothie attempts to achieve.

Items Needed:

Blender(or Smoothie Maker)
Glasses

Ingredients:

1/2 Cup of blueberries
1/2 Cup of strawberries
1/2 Cup of blackberries
1 Medium carrot
1 Cup low-fat milk
1 Cup pomegranate
2 Cups ice
Preparation Instructions:

Place the berries in the blender and pulse for about 20 seconds. Next, place the rest of the ingredients, including the milk(2%, skim, or soy is fine) and pulse again for 60 seconds. When the mix is done, feel free to pour and serve.

Recipe #4: Banana Crunch Smoothie

Going the completely smooth route is perfectly fine, but sometimes you need something with a bit of crunch to it. So, why not add a bit of granola to the mix?

Items Needed:

Blender(or Smoothie Maker)
Glasses

Ingredients:

1 banana
1 cup milk
2 Tbs. of honey or sugar-free honey substitute
1/2 cup granola
1/2 cup of ice

Preparation Instructions:

Blend the ingredients, ensuring that the granola is ground properly and the banana is well sliced. You may use any type of milk you choose, though most will use soy, almond, or skim. Proceed to grind ingredients until mostly smooth.

Recipe #5: Raspberry-Peach Smoothie

Items Needed:

Blender(or Smoothie Maker)
Glasses

Ingredients:

10 oz Frozen Raspberries
1 c Canned Peach Nectar
1/2 c Buttermilk
1 tb Honey

Preparation Instructions:

Thaw the frozen raspberries and cover them completely in syrup. Place ingredients in blender bowl or container, blend until smooth. Serve.

Recipe #6: Basic Protein Smoothie

Items Needed:

Blender(or Smoothie Maker)
Glasses

Ingredients:

1 Banana
2 Strawberries
1 Scoop protein powder
2 Tablespoons sugar or sugar substitute
1 Cup nonfat milk
3/4 cup ice

Preparation Instructions:

Chop banana into slices, then hull your strawberries, ensuring that there are no seeds left behind. Add all ingredients to blender and proceed to puree until mixture is smooth.

Recipe #7: Cherry Vanilla Smoothie

Items Needed:

Blender(or Smoothie Maker)
Glasses

Ingredients:

1 cup Frozen Cherries
1 cup Frozen Strawberries
1 Tbsp ground flax seed
2 small scoops fat free vanilla frozen yogurt
1/2 tsp vanilla extract
1 cup of 100% cranberry juice
1/4 tsp Cinnamon

Preparation Instructions:

Because all ingredients are small enough to place in the blender, feel free to pour them in, using yogurt as your base. Proceed to blend your ingredients until they are fully mixed.

Recipe #8: Basic Apricot Breakfast Smoothie

Items Needed:

Blender(or Smoothie Maker)
Glasses

Ingredients:
1 cup canned apricot halves in light syrup
6 ice cubes
1 cup nonfat plain yogurt
3 tablespoons sugar

Preparation Instructions:

Pour canned apricots into blender along with syrup(in can). Pour in yogurt and ice cubes, top off with sugar. Blend until smooth and ready to eat.

Recipe #9: Pomegranite Smoothie

Items Needed:
Blender(or Smoothie Maker)
Glasses
Ingredients:

2 cups frozen mixed berries
1 cup pomegranate juice
1 medium banana
1/2 cup nonfat cottage cheese
1/2 cup water

Preparation Instructions:

Make sure your banana is properly diced and ready to insert into
blender, then pour your boxes of pomegranite juice, along with cottage
cheese into the blender. Finally, pour in the half cup of water and blend.

Recipe #10: Coffee-Banana Tofu Smoothie

Items Needed:

Blender(or Smoothie Maker)
Glasses

Ingredients:

1 1/4 cups milk
1/2 cup silken tofu,
1 ripe banana
1-2 tablespoons sugar
2 teaspoons instant coffee powder, preferably espresso
2 ice cubes

Preparation Instructions:

Dice banana and insert all ingredients into blender. Puree until ready to serve.

Part 4: Energy Smoothies

If you visit any gas station, or the checkout line at virtually any grocery store, you are undoubtedly going to discover a plethora of energy drinks. Some of these work, some of them do not, and sometimes it can be difficult to determine which is which. What you can be sure of however, is that most of these are nowhere near the picture of health that a good smoothie will paint. This section will cover the different energy smoothies, but before we get started, let's discuss the primary ingredients and the benefit they can add for the average smoothie. Each ingredient has health benefits and can add that extra energy boost to your day whether you need it in the morning, the afternoon, or the late evening hours.

Blueberries -- In many of the smoothie recipes you will find blueberries, even in those that are not specifically designated as 'energy smoothies'. Blueberries happen to be high in antioxidants, fiber, and of course, water. The flavor they add to the average smoothie is undeniable, and the natural sugar will give you a healthy energy boost any time of the day. Combining them with other smoothie ingredients on this list will give you an even greater boost without the health risk we have long associated with the typical energy drink.

Coconut Water -- Many athletes have embraced the idea of coconut water for the post workout recovery. The substance contains electrolytes, and will therefore help to rehydrate your body. When you are just coming off of a workout sessions, you will generally have less energy due to dehydration -- becoming rehydrated will give you a rather impressive and useful energy boost.

Bananas -- Every smoothie needs some type of base, and most people will choose bananas. Not only are they easy to use, they also help to satisfy hunger pangs. In addition to that, bananas help to make your smoothie much more like a milkshake due to the thickness it adds.

Cinnamon -- Cinnamon will definitely add a slight increase in your energy as it is considered a warming herb. In addition to that, it tends to add amazing flavor.

Almonds -- For those who are interested in a rich nutty flavor, Almonds are without a doubt a great source of healthy fats, and if you want to avoid the nutty flavor, you could simply try almond butter. Either way, you will find that almonds add a great source of energy for the long day ahead.

Dark Chocolate -- Almost everyone craves chocolate at some point, and with that being the case, it is no surprise that so many people want to add dark chocolate to their energy smoothies. For obvious reasons dark chocolate will help you to gain energy for the day, and it also contains a great number of antioxidants.

Recipe #1: Basic Energy Smoothie

Items Needed:

Blender(or Smoothie Maker)
Glasses

Ingredients:

1 cup low-fat vanilla yogurt
3/4 cup low-fat milk
3/4 cup fiber rich oatmeal
1/2 grapefruit, juice of
1 whole tangerine (without skin)
1/2 banana
2 teaspoons peanut butter
2 tablespoons vanilla whey protein powder
1 tablespoon honey
4 ice cubes
Direction

Preparation Instructions:

As with any other smoothie recipe, make sure you dice the banana. In addition to that, make sure your yogurt and milk are placed into the blender and mixed until smooth.

Recipe #2: All Day Energy Smoothie

Items Needed:

Blender(or Smoothie Maker)
Glasses

Ingredients:

1 cup ice
1 cup soy milk
1/2 cup fat-free yogurt
3 strawberries
1 banana
1 cup blueberries
1 tablespoon nutritional yeast
1 teaspoon flaxseed oil
1 tablespoon honey

Preparation Instructions:

Core strawberries and ensure all seeds have been removed. Place all ingredients in blender and proceed to pulse for 90 seconds or until smooth.

Recipe #3: Blueberry-Soy Smoothie

Items Needed:

Blender(or Smoothie Maker)
Glasses

Ingredients:

1 cup vanilla soymilk
1 cup firm light tofu
3/4 cup fresh blueberries
2 scoops soy-protein powder
1 tsp almond extract

Preparation Instructions:

Pour soymilk into blender followed by the rest of the ingredients. Once ready, pulse for 45 seconds or until completely smooth. Serve and enjoy.

Recipe #4: Super Energy Smoothie

Items Needed:

Blender(or Smoothie Maker)
Glasses

Ingredients:

1/2 cup orange juice
4 to 6 strawberries
1/2 banana
1/4 cup silken tofu
1 tablespoon honey or sugar
6 ice cubes

Preparation Instructions:

Slice banana and hull strawberries, then blend all ingredients, serve
immediately.

Recipe #5: Cocoa-Peanut Butter Smoothie

Items Needed:

Blender(or Smoothie Maker)
Glasses

Ingredients:

Makes 2 servings
2 tbsp 100% pure cocoa powder
2 tbsp creamy natural peanut butter
1 medium ripe banana
8 oz non-fat vanilla (Greek) yogurt

Preparation Instructions:

Begin by pouring the peanut butter, cocoa powder, and Greek yogurt into the blender. Insert ice cubes and proceed to blend at high speed. One the ingredients are sufficiently blended, proceed to slice the banana, add into mixture, and re-blend. Eventually the mixture will become completely smooth, and at this point you may decide whether or not to add a dash of cinnamon. Pour into glasses and serve immediately.

The Five Day Meal Plan

While having the various recipes might be great, knowing what you can do with them will help you out even more. The following is a five day meal plan. Keep in mind that you can mix and match these for different weeks, and of course insert your own smoothie ideas. The future of taste is in your hands!

Breakfast: Start the week off by checking out recipe #5 under Energy Smoothies. There is nothing quite like an energy drink to start the day, especially one with cocoa powder. After the weekend, you need all the help you can get to start moving! If you feel you don't need an energy drink however, feel free to try one of the other fruit smoothies we mentioned.

Lunch: If you want to get off to a good mid-day, then you might want to look into one of the red lettuce smoothies. Not only are they tasty, they have plenty of nutritional value. There are many other green smoothies on the list, all of which make for a perfect meal replacement – a real winner if you happen to be on the move a lot!

Dinner: While the smoothie is a meal replacement, you can feel free to mix it up a bit with a solid meal so long as you do not cancel out the effects of your smoothie diet.

Solid Meals

Meal 1: Herb Roasted Chicken

2 lbs. bone-in chicken parts, skin removed
4 cups baby carrots
2 large onions

1 tsp. chopped fresh rosemary

2 cups hot cooked brown rice

1/4 tsp. salt

1/8 tsp. black pepper

Oven Temp: 425 (Could vary depending on your Oven

Cook Time: 45 Minutes

Meal 2: Pan-Seared Beef

2 Tbsp. Butter or Spray Butter

1 lb. lean top sirloin steak

2 large shallots or 1 small onion, chopped

1/2 cup non alcoholic dry red wine (or stock)

1/2 cup fat free reduced sodium beef broth

4 medium baked potatoes

8 cups green beans, steamed

Oven Temp: Pan Fry over Medium Heat

Pesto Chicken

2 Tbsp. olive oil

4 boneless, skinless chicken breast halves

4 cups whole-wheat cooked couscous

8 cups steamed green beans

Pesto Sauce Mix

Grill or Boil

Meal 3:

Pasta Salad

8 ounces whole grain or regular bow tie pasta

6 Tbsp. Mayonaise

2 Tbsp. chopped fresh basil or 1 tsp. dried basil leaves

1 clove garlic, finely chopped

1/4 tsp. ground black pepper

2 cans of tuna packed in water, drained and flaked

1 lb frozen green beans, thawed

2 cups cherry tomatoes, quartered OR grape tomatoes, halved

1/3 cup chopped onion

These are three meals that stand entirely apart from your smoothie diet. During the course of the week you will have the opportunity to experiment with a number of different meal replacement options, each of them being a great choice for any time of the day. While they may not seem like much, these smoothies will fill you up and keep you on the go 24/7.

3660735R00054

Printed in Great Britain
by Amazon.co.uk, Ltd.,
Marston Gate.